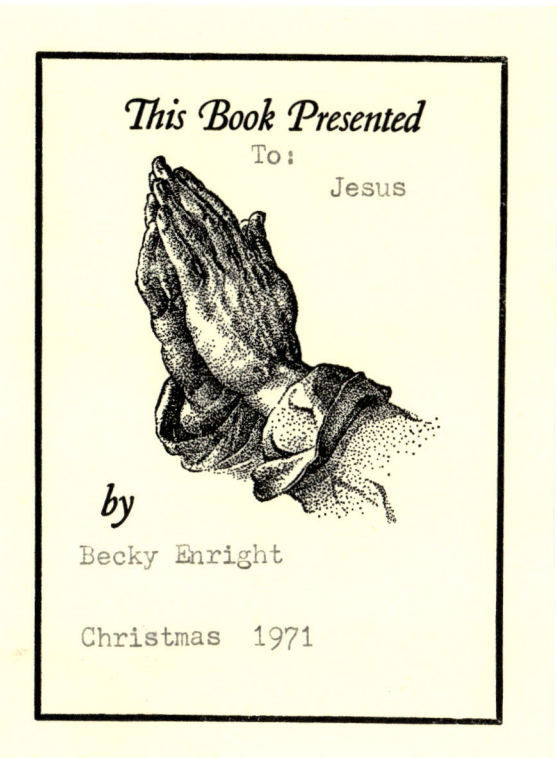

This Book Presented

To:

Jesus

by

Becky Enright

Christmas 1971

THIS BOOK BELONGS TO

MANNERS Don't Come Naturally

By Robert Sylwester

Illustrations by Allan Eitzen

CONCORDIA PUBLISHING HOUSE, ST. LOUIS, MO.

Concordia Publishing House, St. Louis, Missouri
Concordia Publishing House Ltd., London, W. C. 1

Library of Congress Catalog Card No. 64-21139

MANUFACTURED IN THE UNITED STATES OF AMERICA

"IT'S BOBBY'S TURN TO GIVE THE REPORT NEXT WEEK," said Miss Blomkin one Friday afternoon in October. "Bobby, come up here and pick a topic out of the hat."

Everyone waited anxiously to see what would be written on the slip of paper. At the beginning of the year Miss Blomkin wrote the titles for 30 reports on pieces of paper, one for every pupil in the class. Each pupil had one week to prepare his report. During that week he didn't have to do any arithmetic or spelling or anything. He just worked on his report. On Friday afternoon at two o'clock he presented his report to the class. This week's report was a puppet show on "How to Stay Healthy." Last week Mary Johnson used old newspapers, pictures, and maps in presenting a report on "The History of Our Town." The class enjoyed these reports very much. It was fun to spend a week preparing a report, and it was fun to listen to the reports of others.

Bobby put his hand in the hat and felt around. Finally he selected a slip of paper and pulled it out. He unfolded it and laughed as he read, "Good Manners." Everyone else in the room laughed too.

Bobby was the last person you would expect to give a report on good manners. His manners and behavior were anything but good. He ate with his elbows on the table. He teased little children until they cried. He crowded into lines whenever he could. He didn't play fair in games. He didn't act respectful to older people. He didn't comb his hair or wash his face unless someone made him do it. He would talk out loud in school without asking permission. He hardly ever remembered to say "Please" or "Thank you."

Some people couldn't understand why a boy like Bobby could act the way he did. He had good parents and a happy home. Every Sunday the whole family went to Sunday school and church, and they had evening devotions after supper every night. In all these, Bobby heard of God's love to man again and again. He could tell many Bible stories at the drop of a hat – how Jesus came to earth to live among sinful man, how Jesus went about helping people, how Jesus suffered and died for our sins.

You would think that Bobby would be so happy to be a Christian that he would want to show his love to others in everything he did, just as Jesus and his parents showed love to him. He didn't though. He usually thought of himself and his desires first. He thought of others when it didn't take any extra effort.

Good manners and good behavior don't come naturally just because a person has kind parents and attends church and hears a lot of Bible stories. Those things are important, but they're not the whole story. Something else is involved. Bobby would discover that something else during the coming week.

Right now, though, he was facing the results of his bad behavior during recess that morning. Because he had squirted water on several girls during recess, Miss Blomkin had said that he would have to stay after school for half an hour.

After school Miss Blomkin went over to Bobby's desk and sat down. "Do you have any ideas on how to develop your report?" she asked.

"Are you kidding?" he replied. "What do I know about good manners? I wouldn't even know where to start. Can I pick another topic?"

Miss Blomkin told Bobby that she was sure he could develop a very fine report on manners if he put his mind

MNOPQRSTUVW

to it. She suggested that he watch people very carefully during the coming weekend to see how they behave. Then on Monday he could start to look in books and talk to people around school. "Not only will you give a fine report, but I think you will improve your manners in the process," continued Miss Blomkin. "Why not give it a real try anyway?"

"All right, Miss Blomkin, I'll try my best," said Bobby. "Can I go now?"

"*May* I go now?" responded Miss Blomkin. "Yes, Bobby, you *may* go now."

As he ran out the room, he knocked two books off a desk and slammed the door. Miss Blomkin heard him yell, "Get out of my way!" to someone as he ran down the hall. "My, my, that boy certainly has a lot to learn this next week," thought Miss Blomkin as she picked up the books and prepared to plan her lessons for the next week.

"Boy, I sure got out of there easy," thought Bobby as he ran out the front door of the school. He ran right through a game of hopscotch and hollered at the girls when they said they were going to tell on him. He was in a hurry to get to the ball field so he could play with the boys. When he arrived, he discovered they were already playing. They hadn't waited for him.

"Hey, whose side am I on?" he shouted as he ran onto the field.

"Nobody's. We thought you'd have to stay after school for a million hours so we chose up sides and they're even," said one of the boys.

"Why don't you go chase little kids?" said another. "You must think it's fun because you're always doing it." All the boys laughed, and suddenly Bobby found himself blushing. He started to say something in reply, but he noticed that the game had resumed and nobody was paying any attention to him. After a minute or so he walked away, feeling very lonesome.

He walked over to the swings and started to swing by himself. As he swung back and forth, he began to think of why he was all by himself and not with the other boys. He was angry with Miss Blomkin for keeping him after school, and he was angry with the boys for not letting him play. He felt that everyone was against him.

"What's the matter, son, won't anyone play with you?" Bobby looked up and saw Mr. Jackson, the school janitor.

"Can't say I'd blame them the way you've been acting around here," Mr. Jackson continued. "It doesn't take any more effort to be pleasant than it does to be unpleasant. As a matter of fact, I'd say it's much easier to be pleasant and mannerly."

"Oh, go sweep your rooms," growled Bobby. He jumped off the swing and started to walk away.

"I'm proud of my clean rooms, son. When pupils and teachers tell me they like to come to school in the morning because it always looks so clean, why, I feel happy all over. It's one way I can serve my fellowman, and I'm happy to do it. Yes, sir, young fellow, you should know what I'm talking about. You go to church. We Christians have a special reason for wanting to serve our fellowman. You think about that."

Bobby kept walking away, but Mr. Jackson's last words had made an impression. It was true that he always liked to see the clean schoolroom in the morning, even if his own desk was usually messy. He always liked it when his mother put clean sheets on the bed, even if his feet were dirty. He liked to ride in the car just after it had been washed, and he liked to play on a newly mowed lawn. In each case someone had to do some work for his enjoyment. Mr. Jackson was always doing things for others. It embarrassed him to think of all the times he had made Mr. Jackson's work harder by tracking mud into the classroom and things like that.

He reached the street just as Miss Blomkin was leaving school with a load of papers and books. "Good night, Bobby! Have a pleasant weekend," she said.

"G'night," mumbled Bobby. He watched her walk to her car and place her books on the ground so she could open the car door. Then she picked up her things and got in. She smiled and waved at him as she drove off.

"I guess I should have opened the car door for her," thought Bobby.

Bobby was unusually silent at supper that evening. He didn't complain about the food or argue with his brother or sister. In turn everyone was pleasant to him. His father talked about work, and his older brother told about the football game the high school was playing that evening. Bobby was very happy when his father suggested that the whole family go to the game. Before Bobby knew what he was saying, he had volunteered to help his mother and sister do the dishes so they could get started sooner. His mother's "Why, thank you, Bobby!" made him feel better than anything anyone had said to him all day.

While they were doing the dishes, Bobby's mother asked him why he was so quiet. Bobby told her about the assignment Miss Blomkin had given him for the coming week and about all the troubles he had that afternoon. His mother said she was happy to hear he would have to think about good manners for a week. She hoped it would do some good.

"That's just the trouble," said Bobby. "I don't know how to go about studying manners. I don't know what I'm going to write for next Friday."

"Why, that's no problem," responded his mother. "You can begin by watching the behavior of the people at the game this evening. Notice when they use good manners and when they use poor manners. You watch the people and we'll watch the game."

They got to the game early and found good seats. Everyone was in a gay mood. Bobby's mother explained why they sat in the middle of the row of seats instead of at the end. She said it was so that the people who came later could get to seats without bothering the people already seated. She told Bobby to remember that whenever he looked for a seat in church or in a theater. It's an example of good manners because you are thinking of other people before yourself. Bobby noticed that most people in the grandstand were doing just that. As the

AISLE 7

stands began to fill, he noticed confusion only in those rows where the first ones to sit down had taken seats at the end of the row.

"How do you remember all these rules?" asked Bobby.

"What rules?"

"Well, like where you're supposed to sit and all that."

"Those aren't rules, Bobby," his mother answered. "It's just that mannerly people always think what their actions will do to other people. You don't need to memorize a lot of rules to be mannerly. You just keep your eyes open and think of the happiness and welfare of others. That shouldn't be hard for a Christian who knows how God has provided for his happiness and welfare. A Christian will want to make others happy."

She went on, "It is true that people have discovered the best way to do some things, and you might call these rules of behavior. For example, teachers usually ask pupils to raise their hands if they want to say something in class. If teachers didn't have some sort of system about this, several pupils might want to talk at the same time, and it would be difficult to understand any of them."

"I can see that," said Bobby, "even though I guess I don't always do it, but why am I supposed to walk on the street side of the sidewalk when I'm walking with a girl or lady? Why is that the best side?"

"Trying to trick me, aren't you?" his mother laughed. "Some things are called good manners because they have become customs. The one you mentioned goes back to the days before streets were paved. Men walked on the outside so that any mud or dust from passing wagons would land on them instead of the lady. Men still follow this custom even though streets are paved now. Did you notice that Daddy observed this custom this evening on the way to the game? I appreciate it when he does things like that. Learning customs like that doesn't come naturally, Bobby. We have to teach you, and you have to practice until it comes naturally. Say, speaking of customs, here comes one right now."

The band began to play "The Star-Spangled Banner," and everyone stood up. All the men took off their hats. Except for the band, everyone was quiet during the playing unless they were singing along. Bobby thought about this custom. He decided that standing up for the national anthem was one way to show love and respect for your country, and so it would be an example of good manners.

As soon as the band finished playing the national anthem, the people began to shout, and the teams got ready for the kickoff. The two captains came to the center of

the field, talked for a bit, and then shook hands before going back to their teams.

While this was going on, Bobby noticed that some people in the stands were shouting things like "Murder the bums!" and "Go kill 'em, team!" Bobby had heard things like this at other games, but this time it sounded bad. He thought, "How could these people be so mannerly during the playing of "The Star-Spangled Banner" and then holler things like this now?" The players were being mannerly, but some of the spectators were being unmannerly. Bobby remembered what his older brother had said that evening at supper. He told how the coach wanted his players to come to the game dressed in suits and ties to remind them that they are men, so that they would act like men during the game. The coach said that he wanted them to win only if they would win fair and square like gentlemen.

As the game progressed, Bobby noticed that the players on both sides played hard and tackled hard, but that they always helped the tackled man get up. Whenever someone got hurt, players from both sides came running to help.

At the half he went with his father to the snack bar to get some popcorn and cokes for the family. He noticed that most of the people waited patiently in line to be served. Usually he pushed up to the front to get served

76
70
71
74
72
10

first, but he noticed that it took only a few minutes longer if everyone waited in line, and nobody got angry either. Maybe there was something to this manners business after all.

During the second half Bobby spent a lot of time watching the people. His team was winning, so most of the people sitting near them were happy. It bothered him to hear some of the people on the losing side complain that the coach was using the wrong players or using the wrong plays. Some of the people even made bad remarks about the players who dropped passes or got tackled. "Don't those people know that the players are doing their best?" thought Bobby. "They want to win." Then he remembered the many times he said the same things and how he hollered at his teammates when they dropped passes or made mistakes in the games they played at school and in the neighborhood.

Bobby's team won the game, and everyone left for home. During the walk Bobby continued to think about his report on good manners. It interested him more and more. "Everyone thinks I can't make a good report on manners because I have bad manners," he thought. "I'll bet I can write a pretty good report if I try." In bed he decided that he would begin gathering information tomorrow. Next Friday he would surprise Miss Blomkin and the entire class with the best report they had ever heard.

Just before he dozed off he had another idea that would surprise everybody. He laughed to himself. "Wait till they see what else I have up my sleeve. Boy, this is going to be neat!" There was a smile on his face as he fell asleep.

The next morning his mother asked him to return two books to the church. She told him to give them to Pastor Walters and to be sure and say "Thank you." Bobby was glad to go because he wanted to get started on his report, and Pastor Walters was just the person he wanted to see first.

Pastor Walters was working in his office when Bobby got to the church. He greeted Bobby warmly as he took the books and put them on his bookshelf.

"Could I ask you for some help, Pastor Walters?" Bobby suddenly asked.

"Why, yes, Bobby, what is it? Sit down and we'll talk about it."

Bobby told all about his assignment to write a report

on good manners. He asked whether the Bible said anything about manners.

"I should say it does," Pastor Walters replied. "The Bible is much more than a book on manners, but it does tell us how we are to live with our fellowman. You became a special child of God when you were baptized, Bobby. Since that time your parents and your church have spent much time and effort to teach you what it means to be a child of God. For example, do you remember last week's Sunday school lesson?"

"I didn't pay very close attention," confessed Bobby. "I think it was about Peter and John healing a lame man at the temple door, or something like that."

"That's the right story," said Pastor Walters. "The man had been lame from birth and had to beg to get money for food. Peter told him that he didn't have any money to give but that he would give what he had. Then Peter said, 'In the name of Jesus Christ of Nazareth, rise up and walk.' And the man was able to walk for the first time in his whole life."

"Now I have a question for you, Bobby," continued Pastor Walters. "Why do you suppose our church taught you that particular story?"

"I don't know," replied Bobby.

"Well, that's just why you should have paid close attention," said Pastor Walters. "Unless you know the answer to that question, you will never really understand what good behavior and good manners are all about."

"Will you tell me the answer now?" asked Bobby. "I'll promise to listen in Sunday school from now on."

"You and your promises!" laughed Pastor Walters. "Surely I'll tell you. And I'll hold you to your promise too."

They both laughed.

Pastor Walters continued, "It's really quite simple. This story occurred soon after Jesus ascended into heaven. Peter and John knew that Jesus had completed His work on earth and that their salvation was now assured. They were so happy over what Jesus had done for them and everyone else on earth that they wanted to show their happiness by doing everything they could to help others. That's why they were so quick to help the lame man."

"They probably didn't have any money to give the lame man because they had already given all their money away," added Bobby.

"That's possible," said Pastor Walters. "Read the first seven chapters of the Book of Acts sometime, and you will

see just how these early Christians helped one another unselfishly. It puts most of us to shame."

"I just remembered something else from the story," said Bobby. "The rulers put Peter and John in prison after they healed the lame man. Boy, that was surely a dirty trick!"

"Yes, it was, Bobby, but it does show us how willing Peter and John were to help others. They were willing to help others even though they knew it would make the rulers angry enough to put them in prison. The rulers were jealous because the people were listening to the disciples preach instead of to them."

"Now, Bobby, I have another question to ask you," said Pastor Walters. "Can you tell me why Christians want to show happiness by helping other people? Isn't that a rather strange way to show happiness?"

"Because the Bible tells us to do so," suggested Bobby.

"Come on now, Bobby, the Bible is a pretty big book. Where in the Bible?"

"I give up again," said Bobby. "Will you tell me where?"

"Actually, you can find the answer in several places," continued Pastor Walters. "John tells us of one incident in the 13th chapter of his gospel. It happened during the last supper of Jesus and His disciples, just before Judas betrayed Him, and just a day or so before He was crucified. It's possible that the early Christians remembered this incident very clearly because it was one of the last things Jesus told them as a group. Right after Judas left, Jesus said to the remaining eleven disciples: "A new commandment I give to you, that you love one another; even as I have loved you, that you also love one another. By this all men will know that you are My disciples, if you have love for one another" (John 13:34, 35 RSV). So you see, Bobby, it's not a strange way to show happiness by being pleasant and kind and helpful to others. It's the most natural way in the world to a Christian. It's the way Jesus taught us to show happiness. It's hard to imagine how a person could be selfish and unkind if he knew how kind and helpful Jesus was. But some people are."

Bobby was silent.

"I know just what you're thinking," continued Pastor Walters with a twinkle in his eye. "You want to know what all this has to do with good manners and such things as being polite and not slurping your soup."

Bobby laughed. "That's just what I was going to ask. Can't I love other people and still slurp my soup?"

"Yes, Bobby, it's possible to be a Christian and still have poor manners if you don't know your actions offend and annoy other people. But as soon as you find out how people want you to act around them, you will want to change your behavior and adopt these good manners to your way of living. Good manners don't come naturally. They have to be learned and practiced, but the desire to have good manners comes naturally to a Christian."

"Well, why do I have bad manners then?" asked Bobby. "Is it because I'm not a Christian or because I haven't learned what good manners are?"

Pastor Walters laughed, "That's a tough question to answer, Bobby. If I could answer questions like that, I'd be a pretty wise man. About all I can say is that I'm pretty sure that you're a Christian, and I'm pretty sure that your parents have told you all about good manners. Maybe it's because you haven't been keeping your eyes and ears open to what your parents, teachers, and friends have been showing you and telling you about good manners. Pay close attention to what you see and hear this week while you're working on your report. I think maybe you'll discover the answer to your question yourself. Then include it in your report."

"OK, I'll promise to do that, Pastor Walters," said Bobby. "And then I wanted to ask you one more question:

Do any Bible passages tell us what manners and behavior to use?"

"Yes, Bobby, the Bible gives us some clear guides to living. People who love God will want to pattern their life after these guides. Some are quite well known, such as the Ten Commandments and the Golden Rule. I'll tell you what, Bobby, I'll write down several Bible references that you can read and understand. You look these up when you get home, and write them down. I think they will help you understand how God would like to have us express our love to Him and our fellowman."

Pastor Walters took out a piece of paper and wrote down some references. He thought for a minute, scratched his head, opened a big book on his desk, and paged around in it. Then he added some more references to the list. He handed the page to Bobby and smiled.

"Thank you very much, Pastor Walthers," said Bobby as he left the office. He was surprised at himself that he remembered to be polite. He was also somewhat surprised that such a busy man as Pastor Walters would be so kind and willing to help. He blushed to himself as he remembered that he hadn't even helped Miss Blomkin yesterday when she tried to open the car door with an armful of books and papers. He also thought of all the

things his parents did for him even though they were busy, and how he always grumbled when they asked him to do a little errand, even when he wasn't doing anything but playing.

When he got home he went to his room and opened the Bible on his desk. He got out a piece of paper and a pencil and started to look up the Bible passages. Every time he found one, he would write it down on the paper. When he was all done, he had written these passages on the paper:

Ps. 147:1	It is good to sing praises unto our God.
Ps. 26:8	Lord, I have loved the habitation of Thy house and the place where Thine honor dwelleth.
Eccl. 5:1	Keep thy foot when thou goest to the house of God and be more ready to hear than to give the sacrifice of fools.
Col. 3:20	Children, obey your parents in all things, for this is well pleasing unto the Lord.
Lev. 19:32	Thou shalt rise up before the hoary head and honor the face of the old man.
Matt. 22:39	Thou shalt love thy neighbor as thyself.

Eph. 4:32	Be ye kind one to another, tenderhearted, forgiving one another, even as God for Christ's sake hath forgiven you.
James 4:11	Speak not evil one of another, brethren.
Matt. 5:16	Let your light so shine before men that they may see your good works and glorify your Father which is in heaven.
Matt. 7:12	Therefore all things whatsoever ye would that men should do to you, do ye even so to them.
Gal. 6:10	As we have therefore opportunity, let us do good unto all men.

Bobby went downstairs and asked his father to explain some of the words. His father helped him find the words in the dictionary. Then he asked, "Now can you tell me why we should do the things these verses say?"

"Because God tells us to," answered Bobby.

"And . . ."

"Oh, and because I want to," Bobby added hurriedly.

His father laughed, "Yes, don't forget that. It's the most important reason for Christians. Remember what Pastor Walters said about how God leads us into a new life through Baptism. Through Baptism we Christians can appreciate the great things God has done for us. Even though we sin much and don't deserve it, God takes care of our every need. He leads us to faith and keeps us in faith and forgives our sins. Why, Bobby, Christians are naturally so happy about all these wonderful things that they just want to show it by singing their praises to God and by being as kind and helpful to others as they can be. Christians think it's great to live Christian lives. They don't want to live any other kind."

"I'll do my best to remember all this," said Bobby.

"I'm sure you will," responded his father.

That afternoon Bobby was playing football with some neighborhood boys when everyone got into a big fight. Bobby became angry just like the rest of them. It's hard to say who started the argument, because everyone was blaming everyone else. Finally they separated into two groups, but neither group had enough members to play anything that was fun. So they just sat around and told bad things about the boys in the other group. Gradually Bobby's group broke up, and Bobby went home. There wasn't anything to do, so he just went inside and sat on the sofa. After a while his mother asked him why he wasn't playing. Bobby just shrugged.

"Well, then, you can help me clean the house," said his mother. "Here, take this dustcloth and start dusting the furniture."

"Do I have to?" whined Bobby. "I was just going to watch TV."

His mother just said, "Get started," and walked out of the room. Bobby got up after a few minutes and started snapping the cloth at the furniture. He wasn't the least bit interested in doing a good job, and he didn't. When he heard his mother go upstairs, he quickly put the dustcloth back and sneaked outside.

"Bobby, come back here!" It was his mother calling. "I told you to dust the furniture, and you didn't do half of it. Come back here and finish the job." Bobby walked home slowly. By the time he got to the lawn he was angry.

"Why do I always have to do everything? Why can't Jane do some work? All she does is play with her stupid dolls." Bobby gave his younger sister's doll buggy a kick as he walked across the lawn.

"All right, young man, if you're going to act like that, you can sweep the basement and rake the lawn after you finish your dusting," said his mother crossly as she watched him kick the doll buggy.

Bobby took the dustcloth and started to dust again.

He muttered all sorts of bad things under his breath about his mother and work and life in general. It wasn't until he went down to sweep the basement that he began to cool down and think about how he had gotten into such a fix. He laughed to himself as he thought about the other boys who had been playing football. He wondered how many also ended up working around the house. "I guess it's all our own fault," he thought. "If we hadn't started the fight, we'd probably still be playing."

As he continued to sweep, he discovered he wasn't angry with his mother anymore. Actually he was beginning to enjoy sweeping the basement. The basement would be clean now and more fun to play in. He pretended he was a sailor swabbing the deck after a storm.

After he had finished the basement, he went to the garage to get a rake. He noticed his neighbor, Billy Smith, raking leaves in his yard too. Billy had been on the other side during the big argument earlier in the afternoon.

Bobby laughed as he called over, "I see you got stuck with raking leaves too. I guess we should have kept our tempers and played ball instead of fighting."

"I guess you're right," replied Billy. "Hey, I've got an idea. I'm just starting too. Let's help each other, and then maybe we can make a big pile of leaves and have a bonfire tonight."

"Hey, neat!" shouted Bobby. "Maybe we can get all the guys together and roast apples in the fire. If we do a good job, I'll bet our parents will let us have a bonfire. I'll come over and help you first."

That night in bed Bobby thought of all the things that had happened that day. The whole neighborhood had come to the bonfire, and everyone had fun, even the grownups. Pastor Walters had given him some good advice about behavior that morning. It was just too bad that he had forgotten the advice several times during the day. Some of the Bible verses he looked up went through his mind: "Children, obey your parents in all things" . . . "Be ye kind one to another, forgiving" . . . "Speak not evil one of another" . . . "Let us do good to all men." The fight could have been avoided if everyone had played fair, and he could have avoided the argument with his mother if he had been kinder. He felt sorry because of what he had said. After all, she had been working all day, and he had spent much of the day playing. He should have offered to help her.

What was the part Pastor Walters had read about the Last Supper? It was somewhere in the Book of John. He got up and went to his desk and started to page around in his Bible until he found it in the 13th chapter. It was verses 34 and 35 that Pastor Walters had read. He wrote it down and added it to his notes: "A new commandment I give to you that you love one another; even as I have loved you, that you also love one another. By this all men will know that you are My disciples, if you have love for one another."

In his prayers he asked God to forgive his sins and to help him love others more and show his love better.

As Bobby and his family were driving to Sunday school and church, he thought about his manners report again. He decided he would watch the congregation to see what kind of manners people had in church. He watched carefully and wrote down these things when he got home.

1. People dress up for church. Dad says it's because they want to show their respect to God.
2. Almost everyone sings the hymns. I guess singing is another way of showing respect and thanks to God. It doesn't make much sense to go to church to worship and then keep quiet when everyone else is singing, as I saw some people do this morning.
3. Parents try to keep babies and small children quiet during church. Mom says it's difficult for other

people to worship if there is a lot of talking and noise. Most people are willing to put up with noise that babies make, but they expect older children to pay attention and not to talk and play around. I can improve my church behavior.

4. When I told Mr. Sampson that I was going to try to be a better pupil in Sunday school from now on, he said, "Hooray!" I guess I make his job tougher when I fool around. It's hard to teach and it's hard for pupils to learn when some pupils fool around and don't pay attention. Mr. Sampson told me to think of the example of Jesus in the temple when I come to Sunday school and that would remind me how to act.

5. I watched the grownups greet visitors after church. Some visitors didn't get greeted at all, and hardly any of the kids greeted the children the visitors had with them. Greeting visitors is certainly good manners, and not greeting visitors is certainly poor manners. Once Mr. Sampson said that we could do a lot of mission work at our own church each Sunday if we made it a point to greet visitors.

Bobby read what he had written. This would certainly give him some good ideas for his report. He was getting more excited about it every day. "Won't the class and Miss Blomkin be surprised when they discover that this isn't just an ordinary report?" he thought. "Wait till they see the extra surprise I have up my sleeve." He could see their faces now.

Bobby spent much of his time Monday reading about manners in the school library. He found several books that he liked: Munro Leaf's *Manners Can Be Fun;* Tina Lee's *Manners to Grow On;* Sesyle Joslin's *What Do You Say, Dear?* and Eva Evans' *People Are Important.* He also found a lot of material in encyclopedias. He looked up the words "manners" and "etiquette." The word "etiquette" interested him. The encyclopedias said it was a French word meaning "keep off the grass." The encyclopedias also explained how that word came to mean manners in English. He decided that other children would also be interested in the story of this word if they would look up "etiquette" in their encyclopedias.

That evening Bobby asked his mother for a list of manners from mothers. She replied that her list would probably be about a thousand pages long. Then she

BOOK LISTS

laughed and said that all she really wanted could be said in a few words – that the whole family love each other as much as she loved them, and that's a whole lot. What really hurt her was to see any of them being mean to someone else. She added that she made house rules from time to time, but that was so they would know how to show their love for each other. She said that she liked being a mother because it gave her a chance to teach her children how to show Christian love for others. This meant that her children would disappoint her at times, but she hoped they would show love for others in everything they did by the time they grew up and left home. Then she laughed and said that Bobby, at the rate he was learning, would probably have to stay at home until he was 85 years old.

Bobby blushed, and his mother went over to him and hugged him. That just made him blush more. His mother said, "I'm sorry, Bobby. I just wanted to tease you a bit. And I only tease people I love. Let's look at your list of manners."

"Here they are," said Bobby. "These are things you always tell us. I guess I would feel the same way if I had to do the cooking and cleaning."

1. Make sure your shoes are clean when you come into the house.

2. Be happy and show it when you eat meals. Tell your mother if you like the meal, and don't complain all the time if you don't.

3. Don't throw your clothes on the floor, and don't throw yourself on the furniture.

Bobby's mother laughed again when she saw the list. She said she had some more things she could add, but that she would settle for these if everyone would promise to do that much. "But do it because you want to, not because you have to," she added.

Bobby's father came into the room and looked at the list. He took out his pen and added two more. They all laughed when they saw what he wrote:

4. Help your mother all you can so there won't be any work left for me to do when I get home from work.

5. Laugh at all my jokes.

Tuesday morning Bobby went to see Mrs. Frank, the cook in the school cafeteria. He told her about his report and asked what suggestions she could give for table manners.

"Why, Bobby, I could give you all sorts of suggestions. Make sure your hands and face are washed. Don't talk while you have food in your mouth. Don't stuff your mouth full of food. Ask people please to pass food that you can't reach easily. Talk about pleasant things at meals. But I'm sure that you've heard all these before, and you know how much more pleasant it is to eat when everyone practices these good table manners."

Mrs. Frank continued, "The most important thing I can say, though, is that you should remember that you ask Jesus to be your dinner Guest every time you pray before eating. Imagine, Jesus at your table! What a wonderful honored Guest! Why, this should make every meal an enjoyable experience, a festival occasion. And don't forget that the honored Guest also provided the food. Jesus isn't there to spy on your table manners. He comes because you invited Him and because He likes to be with you. Mealtime should be such a happy time that you would want to practice the table manners your parents are teaching you."

"Thank you, Mrs. Frank," said Bobby. "I never thought of table manners that way before."

Miss Blomkin asked Bobby to come up to her desk just before the end of the school day. "Bobby, do you realize that I haven't had to write your name on the board or ask you to behave once this week?"

Bobby laughed a little. "I guess it's because I've been too busy writing my report on manners to be unmannerly."

"That might be the reason," continued Miss Blomkin. "People who keep themselves busy rarely have time for mischief. Isn't it more fun to keep busy with projects like your report instead of getting into trouble all the time?"

"I guess it is," answered Bobby, "but I'll bet I still get into trouble once in a while."

"Well, I imagine you will. You wouldn't be Bobby if you didn't get into mischief once in a while. But I surely like you better this way," laughed Miss Blomkin.

By Wednesday evening Bobby had pages and pages of notes. He had asked many different people for suggestions. The librarian told him that people come to the library to study and read and that's why libraries should be quiet. Bobby told her he certainly appreciated it that the library was quiet when he was looking up things during the week.

He talked to a policeman for a long time. The policeman reminded him that laws are meant to help people just like good manners. People should find out what the laws are and then do what the laws say. That way people will know how they can serve their fellowman, and everyone will be happier. He also told Bobby that boys and girls should pay particular attention to traffic lights and the rules each city has for bicycle riding. He said that grownups worry about injuring children when they drive. That's why they appreciate it so much when they see a child driving his bicycle properly or crossing streets properly.

Bobby also had a long talk with his older brother and younger sister. All three benefited from the talk. They settled several things which had caused arguments in the past. Bobby thought it would be a good idea if brothers and sisters would talk about their manners with each other from time to time. Sometimes we annoy other people without meaning to. He also discovered that it's important to have good manners around people you're with a lot.

Firemen, milkmen, uncles, aunts, doctors, mailmen, and classmates all added suggestions. Bobby kept his eyes and ears wide open and his pencil busy all week. By Thursday morning he had written so many manners and rules and notes that he didn't know what to do. Miss Blomkin

RESTAURANT

suggested that he take all his notes to the library and read through them carefully to see if he couldn't find a few simple general things to say which everyone could remember instead of pages and pages of rules. She also suggested that he write his report in an interesting manner so that the class would listen attentively.

"Don't worry, Miss Blomkin," said Bobby. "They won't *ever* forget this report."

It took Bobby several hours to read through his notes and to decide what he would say. As Miss Blomkin had suggested, he discovered it took only a few sentences to say everything he had in his pages and pages of notes. Then he remembered that Pastor Walters and his parents had also told him that good manners don't come from a lot of rules but from a simple feeling which comes from the heart.

Bobby wrote his report on Thursday afternoon. He also made a special secret trip to the school office to arrange his surprise. He didn't want anyone in the class to find out what he had in mind. He laughed to himself as he thought about the trick he was playing on his classmates.

The more he thought about it, though, the more he thought that Miss Blomkin had also played a trick on him. Only once during this week she had to ask him to behave, and that was during recess. He also enjoyed school this week more than ever before. He also remembered that he had helped his mother do the dishes every night without grumbling, and that things seemed much more pleasant at home when he wasn't getting into trouble.

Everyone in the class was looking forward to his report on good manners. Some of them said that they wouldn't miss hearing it for a million dollars. Bill Smith said that he would come to school in an ambulance if he got sick on Friday just to hear Bobby give a talk on good manners.

"They'll really be surprised when they see what I have cooked up for them," thought Bobby as he completed his report.

At two o'clock on Friday afternoon Miss Blomkin told the class that they had a special treat today. Several of the boys laughed. She went on to say that Bobby had completed his famous investigation into good manners and he would now give his report.

The class groaned when Bobby got up with a whole

handful of papers. "Boy, that looks like about thirty pages. Are you going to read all that?" asked Bill Smith.

"No, Bill, but this is my report, and it is thirty pages, one page for every one of you," answered Bobby. "Every page is the same. The school secretary printed a copy of my one-page report for each of you. Everything I have to say about good manners will be found on this one page." With that Bobby passed a copy of his report to every member of the class. He continued, "All you have to do is read it. I'm *sure* you all can read, can't you?"

"Hey, is this some kind of joke?" asked Harry Jones.

"Is it written in Chinese?" asked Mary Todd.

"Looks like a combination of Russian, German, and Greek to me," said Bill Smith.

"I'll bet it's in code," suggested Tim Workman.

"Tim's right," said Bobby. "It's in code. If you want to read my report on good manners, you'll have to figure out the code and translate what I wrote."

"Well, I surely want to find out what Bobby has to say about good manners," said Jane Franklin. "Let's get to work."

The whole class agreed, and Bobby walked back to his seat with a big smile on his face.

A B C D E F G H I J K

Miss Blomkin faced the class. "This is certainly different from what we expected, isn't it? Before we begin, perhaps we should spend a few minutes discussing codes so that we can figure this code out. Can anyone tell me something about codes?" Several hands went up, and pupils volunteered to explain codes they knew. Miss Blomkin wrote these suggestions on the board to see if any would unravel Bobby's code. This is what she wrote:

1. Write the next letter of the alphabet instead of the letter in the word, such as b for a, and c for b. *Please come home* would be written *Qmfbtf dpnf ipnf.*

2. Write the letter of the alphabet coming just before the letter meant, such as a for b, and b for c. *Please come home* would be written *Okdzrd bnld gnld.*

3. Turn the letters of the word around. *Please come home* would be written *Esaelp emoc emoh.*

4. Write the whole sentence backwards. *Please come home* would be written *Emoh emoc esaelp.*

5. Reverse the first and last letters of each word. *Please come home* would be written *Eleasp eomc eomh.*

Suddenly Andy White, who had been quiet during the discussion, raised his hand. "I just figured out the code, and it's one of the five on the board." The class immediately wanted to know which one. "I won't tell you," answered Andy, "but it's easy to figure it out if you try out each one on the first few words." In a minute or two everyone figured out which code Bobby had used.

They all worked fast to decode Bobby's report. They wrote the correct word above each code word. Judy Noll finished first. It took her 20 minutes. By 3 o'clock everyone in the room had solved it. Can you do it faster than Miss Blomkin's class? His report is written in code below.

DOOG SRENNAM

Elpoep ohw evah doog srennam era tnasaelp ot eb htiw esuaceb yeht od rieht tseb ot ekam srehto yppah. Snaitsirhc tnaw ot pleh srehto dna ekam meht yppah esuaceb s'that eht yaw ot wohs evol ot srehto. Yeht evol srehto esuaceb yeht era os yppah revo s'tsirhC evol ot meht.

Neve hguoht ew yam tnaw ot wohs ruo evol ot srehto hguorht ruo roivaheb, ew esu dab srennam semitemos.

Doog srennam t'nod emoc yllarutan. Tsom elpeop lliw esucxe seibab fi yeht evah dab elbat srennam dna sgniht ekil taht esuaceb yeht t'nevah denrael tey how elpoep tca. Tub yeht tcepxe redlo nerdlihc ot evah doog srennam tsom fo eht emit esuaceb yeht evah neeb dlot woh ot evaheb. Laer snaitsirhC evah eht evol taht sdael ot doog srennam tub yeht tsum nrael dna ecitcarp eht syaw ni hcihw elpoep wohs rieht evol ot srehto. S'taht yhw naitsirhC nerdlihc tnaw ot nrael dna ecitcarp doog srennam.

Eht tsedrah secalp ot evah doog srennam era ta emoh dna ta loohcs. Ew era htiw ruo ylimaf dna setamloohcs os hcum taht ew semitemos tegrof tuoba meht dna ekat meht rof detnarg. Esuaceb fo siht dna esuaceb ew yllausu evol meht yllaiceps ew dluohs eb artxe luferac ot wohs ruo evol ot meht htiw doog srennam.

Ym srennam t'nevah neeb oot doog ni eht tsap esuaceb

I t'ndid yap hcum noitnetta ot tahw rehto elpoep thguoht fo ym roivaheb. I sseug I t'ndid evol meht hguone ot erac. I ma demahsa fo siht esuaceb I wonk woh hcum doG serac rof em. Fi enoyreve dluow kniht fo eht ssenippah fo srehto, eht dlrow dluow eb a hcum recin ecalp ot evil ni. Enoyreve strats htiw em dna uoy. I esimorp ot yrt ot evol srehto erom dna wohs ym evol retteb.

DO YOU THINK HE WILL??

WILL YOU??

MY MANNERS WORKLIST

MY MANNERS WORKLIST

MY MANNERS WORKLIST

MY MANNERS WORKLIST

Other Books on Manners Noted in Text

Joslin, Sesyle	*What Do You Say, Dear?* (Scott, 1958)
Leaf, Munro	*Manners Can Be Fun* (Lippincott, 1958)
Lee, Tina	*Manners to Grow On* (Doubleday, 1955)
Evans, Eva	*People Are Important* (Capitol, 1951)